HTML AND CSS DEMYSTIFIED

THE WEB DESIGNER'S SECRET WEAPON

OLIVER LUCAS JR

Preface

Have you ever looked at a stunning website and wondered, "Howdid they *do* that?" The intricate layouts, the vibrant colors, the seamless interactions – it can seem like magic. But behind every beautiful website lies the power of code, specifically HTML and CSS.

This book, "HTML & CSS Demystified: The Web Designer's Secret Weapon," is your guide to unlocking that magic. Whether you're a complete beginner taking your first steps into the world of web development or an aspiring designer looking to enhance your skills, this book will equip you with the knowledge and confidence to craft your own captivating online experiences.

We'll embark on a journey through the fundamentals of HTML, building a solid foundation with the essential elements that give structure and meaning to web pages. Then, we'll delve into the art of CSS, exploring the vast array of styling options that bring your creations to life. From typography and colors to layout and responsiveness, you'll learn how to wield CSS as your creative tool, transforming simple code into visually stunning websites.

This book is more than just a dry technical manual. We'll focus on practical application, providing clear explanations, engaging examples, and hands-on exercises that empower you to build real-world projects. You'll learn how to:

Craft the backbone of any website with HTML.

Style your creations with the magic of CSS.

Master the art of responsive design for a seamless mobile experience.

Unleash your creativity with advanced CSS techniques.

By the end of this book, you'll not only understand the "how" but also the "why" behind web design. You'll be equipped to create websites that are not only visually appealing but also user-friendly, accessible, and optimized for performance.

So, are you ready to unlock the web and become a confident web designer? Let's begin!

TABLE OF CONTENTS

Chapter 1

1.1 What is HTML and why is it essential?
1.2 Understanding the role of CSS in web design.
1.3 Setting up your development environment.

Chapter 2

2.1 Exploring basic HTML elements (headings, paragraphs, images).
2.2 Working with lists (ordered and unordered).
2.3 Creating links and navigation.

Chapter 3

3.1 Selectors: Targeting HTML elements with CSS.
3.2 Properties and values: Modifying the appearance of elements.
3.3 CSS Units: Understanding pixels, percentages, and ems.

Chapter 4

4.1 The Box Model: Content, padding, border, and margin
4.2 Display property: Inline, block, and inline-block.
4.3 Positioning elements: Static, relative, absolute, and fixed.

Chapter 5

5.1 Font families and web safe fonts
5.2 Text properties: Size, weight, style, and color.
5.3 Line height, letter spacing, and text alignment.

Chapter 6

6.1 Color theory and web color palettes.
6.2 Background colors, images, and gradients.
6.3 Opacity and transparency effects.

Chapter 7

7.1 Image formats: JPEG, PNG, and GIF.
7.2 Image attributes: Alt text, width, and height.
7.3 Responsive images: Adapting to different screen sizes.

Chapter 8

8.1 Media queries: Targeting different devices.
8.2 Fluid layouts and flexible images.
8.3 Mobile-first design principles.

Chapter 9

9.1 Creating forms with various input types.
9.2 Form styling and validation.
9.3 Handling user data with server-side scripting (brief overview).

Chapter 10

10.1 CSS frameworks: Bootstrap and Foundation.
10.2 CSS preprocessors: Sass and Less
10.3 Animations and transitions

Chapter 1

Unlocking the Web: Introduction to HTML & CSS

1.1 What is HTML and why is it essential?

What is HTML?

HTML stands for **HyperText Markup Language**.[1] It's the code that forms the foundation of every single web page you see on the internet.[2] Think of it as the skeleton that provides structure and meaning to the content of a website.[3]

Instead of using complex programming logic, HTML uses a system of **tags** to tell web browsers how to display content.[4] These tags are simple words enclosed in angle brackets, like `<p>` for paragraph, `<h1>` for a main heading, or `<img>` for an image.

Why is HTML Essential?

1 Foundation of the Web: Without HTML, web browsers wouldn't know how to display text, images, videos, or any other content.[5] It's the fundamental language that makes the web work.

2 Structure and Semantics: HTML tags not only tell browsers how to display content but also provide meaning and structure to that content.[6] This is crucial for:

Accessibility: People with disabilities rely on screen readers and other assistive technologies that use HTML structure to understand web page content.[7]

SEO (Search Engine Optimization): Search engines use HTML tags to understand the content and relevance of web pages, which helps them rank higher in search results.[8]

3 Easy to Learn: HTML is relatively easy to learn compared to other programming languages.[9] Its syntax is straightforward, and there are tons of resources available to help beginners get started.[10]

4 Universally Supported: All web browsers understand HTML, ensuring that your web pages can be accessed by anyone, anywhere, regardless of the device they're using.[11]

5 Building Block for Other Technologies: HTML is the foundation upon which other web technologies, like CSS (for styling) and JavaScript (for interactivity), are built.[12]

In essence, HTML is the backbone of the web, providing the structure and meaning that make websites accessible, understandable, and functional for everyone.[13]

1.2 Understanding the role of CSS in web design.

CSS, or Cascading Style Sheets, is like the magic wand of web design. While HTML provides the basic structure and content of a web page, CSS is what brings it to life visually.[1] It's responsible for everything you see and experience on a website in terms of appearance:[2]

Here's a breakdown of CSS's key roles in web design:

1 Visual Presentation: CSS controls the visual aspects of every element on a web page.[3] This includes:

Typography: Font families, sizes, colors, styles (bold, italic), line heights, and spacing.[4]

Colors: Background colors, text colors, borders, gradients, and opacity.[5]

Layout: Positioning elements on the page, creating columns, controlling the flow of content, and designing responsive layouts that adapt to different screen sizes.[6]

Visual Effects: Adding shadows, rounded corners, animations, and transitions to make web pages more dynamic and engaging.[7]

2 User Experience (UX): CSS plays a crucial role in enhancing the user experience by:

Readability: Ensuring text is legible and easy to read by controlling font choices, sizes, and spacing.[8]

Navigation: Styling menus and navigation elements to be clear, intuitive, and user-friendly.[9]

Visual Hierarchy: Using CSS to emphasize important content and guide the user's eye through the page.[10]

Branding: Applying consistent styles to create a cohesive brand identity across the website.[11]

3 Efficiency and Maintainability:

Separation of Concerns: CSS keeps the presentation (styling) separate from the content (HTML), making it easier to update the design without affecting the structure of the website.[12]

Reusability: Styles can be defined once and applied to multiple elements or even across entire websites, saving time and effort.[13]

Consistency: CSS ensures a consistent look and feel across all pages of a website, creating a unified and professional experience.[14]

4 Accessibility:

Visual Impairment: CSS can be used to increase font sizes, adjust color contrasts, and create layouts that are easier to navigate for users with visual impairments.[15]

Other Disabilities: CSS can also be used to improve the experience for users with other disabilities, such as those who use screen readers or have motor impairments.[16]

In short, CSS is essential for transforming a plain HTML document into a visually appealing, user-friendly, and effective website.[17] It empowers web designers to control every aspect of a website's presentation and create engaging experiences for users.[18]

1.3 Setting up your development environment.

Setting up your development environment is the first crucial step to becoming a web developer. It's essentially creating the workspace where you'll write your HTML and CSS code and see your web pages come to life. Here's a breakdown of the process:

1. Choose a Code Editor:

A code editor is where you'll write your HTML and CSS. There are many excellent options available, both free and paid. Some popular choices include:

VS Code (Visual Studio Code): A free, highly customizable, and powerful editor with a vast library of extensions.

Sublime Text: A fast and lightweight editor with a clean interface.

Atom: A free, open-source editor developed by GitHub, known for its flexibility.

Notepad++: A simple and free editor for Windows.

Brackets: A free, open-source editor focused on web development.

2. Install a Web Browser:

You'll need a web browser to view your HTML and CSS creations. Some popular options are:

Google Chrome: Known for its speed, developer tools, and wide range of extensions.

Mozilla Firefox: A strong focus on privacy and open-source development.

Microsoft Edge: The default browser for Windows, built on the Chromium engine.

Safari: The default browser for Apple devices.

3. Create a Project Folder:

Organize your work by creating a dedicated folder on your computer to store your HTML, CSS, and other project files.

4. Write Your First HTML File:

Open your code editor.

Create a new file and save it as `index.html` in your project folder.

Type the basic HTML structure:

HTML

```
<!DOCTYPE html>
<html lang="en">
```

```
<head>
    <meta charset="UTF-8">
                            <meta       name="viewport"
content="width=device-width, initial-scale=1.0">1
    <title>My First Web Page</title>
</head>
<body>
    <h1>Hello, World!</h1>
</body>
</html>2
```

5. View Your HTML File in the Browser:

Open your web browser.

Go to `File` > `Open File` (or a similar option).

Select the `index.html` file from your project folder.

You should now see your "Hello, World!" heading displayed in the browser!

6. Add CSS (Optional):

Create a new file in your project folder and save it as `style.css`.

In your `index.html` file, add a `<link>` tag within the `<head>` section to connect your HTML to your CSS:

HTML

```
<link rel="stylesheet" href="style.css">
```

Now you can start adding CSS rules to `style.css` to style your web page.

Tips for Your Development Environment:

Keep Your Software Updated: Regularly update your code editor, web browser, and any extensions to benefit from the latest features and security updates.

Explore Developer Tools: Modern web browsers have powerful developer tools that allow you to inspect code, debug issues, and analyze performance.

Use Online Resources: Websites like W3Schools, MDN Web Docs, and freeCodeCamp offer comprehensive tutorials and documentation for HTML and CSS.

Practice Regularly: The best way to learn web development is by practicing consistently. Start with small projects and gradually increase complexity.

By following these steps, you'll have a solid foundation for your web development journey. Happy coding!

Chapter 2

Building Blocks of the Web: HTML Fundamentals

2.1 Exploring basic HTML elements (headings, paragraphs, images).

These are the fundamental building blocks you'll use to create the content and structure of your web pages. Let's explore each one:

1. Headings

Headings are used to structure the content of your web page by defining different levels of headings. There are six levels, from `<h1>` (the most important) to `<h6>` (the least important).

Syntax: `<h1>This is a heading</h1>`

Example:

HTML

```
<h1>This is the main heading</h1>
<h2>This is a subheading</h2>
<h3>This is a sub-subheading</h3>
```

Purpose:

Provide a clear hierarchy and organization to your content.

Make your content easier to read and scan.

Improve SEO by signaling to search engines what your page is about.

2. Paragraphs

Paragraphs are used to group related sentences into blocks of text.

Syntax: `<p>This is a paragraph of text.</p>`

Example:

HTML

```
<p>This is the first paragraph of my web page. It contains some important information.</p>
<p>This is the second paragraph, which provides more details.</p>
```

Purpose:

Break up large chunks of text into manageable units.

Improve readability and visual appeal.

3. Images

Images are used to add visual content to your web pages.

Syntax: `<img src="image.jpg" alt="Image description">`

Example:

HTML

```
<img src="my-profile-picture.jpg" alt="My profile picture">
```

Attributes:

`src`: Specifies the URL or path to the image file.

`alt`: Provides alternative text that describes the image, which is important for accessibility and SEO.

Purpose:

Enhance the visual appeal of your web pages.

Convey information more effectively.

Create a more engaging user experience.

Important Notes:

Closing Tags: Most HTML elements require a closing tag (e.g., `</p>`, `</h1>`).

Nesting: You can nest elements inside each other to create more complex structures (e.g., a heading inside a paragraph).

Attributes: Many HTML elements have attributes that provide additional information about the element (e.g., the `src` and `alt` attributes for images).

By mastering these basic HTML elements, you'll be well on your way to creating structured and engaging web pages.

2.2 Working with lists (ordered and unordered).

Lists are incredibly useful for organizing and presenting information on web pages. HTML provides two main types of lists: ordered and unordered.

1. Unordered Lists (`<ul>`):

Purpose: Used to create a list of items where the order doesn't matter.

Syntax:

HTML

```
<ul>

    <li>Item 1</li>

    <li>Item 2</li>

    <li>Item 3</li>

</ul>
```

Output: Each item is displayed with a bullet point by default.

Item 1

Item 2

Item 3

2. Ordered Lists (`<ol>`):

Purpose: Used to create a list of items where the order is important.

Syntax:

HTML

```
<ol>
   <li>First step</li>
   <li>Second step</li>
   <li>Third step</li>
</ol>
```

Output: Each item is displayed with a number by default.

First step

Second step

Third step

Key Concepts:

List Item Element (`<li>`): Both ordered and unordered lists use the `<li>` (list item) element to define each item within the list.

Nesting: You can nest lists within each other to create hierarchical structures. For example, you could have an unordered list of categories, and within each category, an ordered list of steps.

Customization with CSS:

While HTML provides the basic structure for lists, CSS allows you to customize their appearance extensively. You can:

Change bullet styles: Use the `list-style-type` property to change the bullet style in unordered lists (e.g., circles, squares, discs).

Change numbering styles: Use the `list-style-type` property to change the numbering style in ordered lists (e.g., numbers, letters, Roman numerals).

Control spacing and indentation: Use properties like `margin`, `padding`, and `list-style-position` to adjust the spacing and indentation of list items.

Add background colors and images: Use background properties to style the appearance of list items.

Examples:

Navigation Menu: Unordered lists are often used to create navigation menus on websites.

Step-by-Step Instructions: Ordered lists are ideal for presenting step-by-step instructions or procedures.

Product Features: Unordered lists can be used to highlight key features of a product.

Table of Contents: Ordered lists can be used to create a table of contents for a document or web page.

By understanding how to use ordered and unordered lists effectively, you can present information in a clear, organized, and visually appealing way.

2.3 Creating links and navigation.

Links and navigation are essential for creating a user-friendly and interconnected web experience. They allow users to move seamlessly between different pages within your website and to external resources on the internet. Here's how to create links and navigation using HTML:

1. The Anchor Element (`<a>`):

The `<a>` element (short for "anchor") is the foundation for creating links in HTML. It has the following basic syntax:

HTML

```
<a href="target_URL">Link text</a>
```

`href` **attribute:** This is the most important attribute. It specifies the URL (web address) that the link should point to.

Link text: This is the visible text or content that users will click on to follow the link.

2. Types of Links:

Absolute Links: Point to a full web address, including the protocol (http:// or https://) and domain name.

Example: `<a href="https://www.google.com">Go to Google</a>`

Relative Links: Point to another file within your website, relative to the current page's location.

Example: `<a href="about.html">About Us</a>` (links to a page named "about.html" in the same directory)

Example: `<a href="../contact.html">Contact</a>` (links to a page named "contact.html" one level up in the directory structure)

Email Links: Used to create links that open the user's email client.

Example: `<a href="mailto:someone@example.com">Send Email</a>`

3. Navigation with Lists and the `<nav>` Element:

Navigation menus are typically created using a combination of unordered lists (`<ul>`) and the `<nav>` element. The `<nav>` element is a semantic element that defines a section of a page intended for navigation.

HTML

```
<nav>
  <ul>
    <li><a href="index.html">Home</a></li>
    <li><a href="about.html">About</a></li>
    <li><a href="services.html">Services</a></li>
    <li><a href="contact.html">Contact</a></li>[1]
  </ul>
</nav>
```

4. Target Attribute:

The `target` attribute specifies where the linked document should open:

`_blank`: Opens the link in a new browser tab or window.

`_self`: Opens the link in the same frame as it was clicked (default).

`_parent`: Opens the link in the parent frame.

`_top`: Opens the link in the full body of the window.

Example: `<a href="https://www.example.com" target="_blank">Open in new tab</a>`

5. Tips for Effective Navigation:

Keep it Simple: Use clear and concise link text.

Visual Hierarchy: Use CSS to style your navigation and make it visually appealing and easy to use.

Consistency: Maintain a consistent navigation structure across all pages of your website.

Accessibility: Ensure your navigation is accessible to users with disabilities (e.g., use proper semantic elements, provide keyboard navigation, and sufficient color contrast).

By mastering these techniques, you can create effective navigation that enhances the user experience and helps visitors easily find the information they need on your website.

Chapter 3

Styling with CSS: Introducing CSS Syntax

3.1 Selectors: Targeting HTML elements with CSS.

CSS selectors are the key to targeting specific HTML elements and applying styles to them. They act as a bridge between your CSS rules and the content of your web page. Here's a breakdown of the main types of selectors:

1. Type Selectors (Element Selectors):

Target: Select all elements of a specific type (tag name).

Syntax: `elementName { /* CSS rules */ }`

Example: `p { color: blue; }` (targets all `<p>` elements)

2. Class Selectors:

Target: Select elements that have a specific class attribute.

Syntax: `.className { /* CSS rules */ }`

Example: `.highlight { background-color: yellow; }` (targets all elements with `class="highlight"`)

How to use: Add the class attribute to HTML elements: `<p class="highlight">This text is highlighted.</p>`

3. ID Selectors:

Target: Select a single element with a specific ID attribute.

Syntax: `#idName { /* CSS rules */ }`

Example: `#main-heading { font-size: 2em; }` (targets the element with `id="main-heading"`)

How to use: Add the ID attribute to an HTML element: `<h1 id="main-heading">Welcome!</h1>`

Important: IDs should be unique within a single HTML document.

4. Universal Selector:

Target: Selects all elements on the page.

Syntax: `* { /* CSS rules */ }`

Example: `* { margin: 0; padding: 0; }` (resets default margins and padding for all elements)

5. Attribute Selectors:

Target: Select elements based on the presence or value of a specific attribute.

Syntax:

`[attribute]` (selects elements with the attribute)

`[attribute="value"]` (selects elements with the attribute and the specified value)

`[attribute*="value"]` (selects elements with the attribute containing the specified value)

Example: `a[href^="https"] { color: green; }` (targets links that start with "https")

6. Descendant Combinator:

Target: Select elements that are descendants of another element.

Syntax: `ancestor descendant { /* CSS rules */ }`

Example: `ul li { list-style-type: circle; }` (targets all `<li>` elements that are descendants of a `<ul>` element)

7. Child Combinator:

Target: Select elements that are direct children of another element.

Syntax: `parent > child { /* CSS rules */ }`

Example: `nav > ul { background-color: lightgray; }` (targets only the `<ul>` that is a direct child of the `<nav>` element)

These are some of the most common CSS selectors. By understanding how to use them effectively, you can precisely target the elements you want to style and create complex and visually appealing web designs.

3.2 Properties and values: Modifying the appearance of elements.

CSS properties and values are the dynamic duo that let you modify the appearance of HTML elements.[1] Think of properties as the *what* you want to change (e.g., color, size, position) and values as the *how* (e.g., red, 16px, center).

Here's a breakdown of some common CSS properties and their values:

1. Color

`color`: Sets the color of the text content of an element.

Values: Color names (e.g., red, blue, green), hexadecimal codes (e.g., #ff0000), RGB values (e.g., rgb(255, 0, 0)), HSL values (e.g., hsl(0, 100%, 50%)).

background-color: Sets the background color of an element.

Values: Same as color.

2. Font

font-family: Specifies the font family for the text.

Values: Font names (e.g., Arial, Helvetica, Times New Roman), generic font families (e.g., serif, sans-serif, monospace).

font-size: Sets the size of the font.

Values: Absolute units (e.g., px, pt, cm), relative units (e.g., em, rem, %).

font-weight: Sets the weight (boldness) of the font.

Values: Keywords (normal, bold, bolder, lighter), numerical values (100-900).

`font-style`: Sets the style of the font.

Values: `normal`, `italic`, `oblique`.

3. Text

`text-align`: Aligns the text within an element.

Values: `left`, `center`, `right`, `justify`.

`line-height`: Sets the vertical spacing between lines of text.

Values: Numbers (unitless, px, em, etc.), percentages.

`text-decoration`: Adds decorations to the text.

Values: `none`, `underline`, `overline`, `line-through`.

4. Margin and Padding

`margin`: Sets the space outside an element's border.

Values: Length units (px, em, etc.), percentages, keywords (`auto`).

Can be set for individual sides (`margin-top`, `margin-right`, `margin-bottom`, `margin-left`) or all sides at once (`margin`).

padding: Sets the space inside an element's border.

Values: Same as margin.

Can be set for individual sides (padding-top, padding-right, padding-bottom, padding-left) or all sides at once (padding).

5. Border

border: A shorthand property to set all border properties at once.

Values: border-width, border-style, border-color.

border-width: Sets the width of the border.

Values: Length units (px, em, etc.), keywords (thin, medium, thick).

border-style: Sets the style of the border.

Values: none, solid, dotted, dashed, etc.

border-color: Sets the color of the border.

Values: Same as color.

6. Display

`display`: Specifies how an element is displayed.

Values: `block`, `inline`, `inline-block`, `none`, `flex`, `grid`, etc.

Example:

CSS

```css
p {
  color: #333;
  font-family: Arial, sans-serif;
  font-size: 16px;
  line-height: 1.5;
  margin-bottom: 20px;
  padding: 10px;
  border: 1px solid #ccc;
}
```

This CSS code styles all paragraph elements with a dark gray color, Arial font (or a sans-serif fallback), 16px font size, 1.5 line height, 20px bottom margin, 10px padding, and a light gray solid border.

By understanding these properties and values, you can control the visual presentation of your web pages and create engaging and user-friendly designs.

3.3 CSS Units: Understanding pixels, percentages, and ems.

CSS uses a variety of units to specify sizes, lengths, and other measurements. Understanding these units is crucial for creating precise and responsive layouts. Here's a breakdown of pixels, percentages, and ems:

1. Pixels (px)

Definition: Pixels are absolute units that represent a single dot on a computer screen.

Usage: Pixels are commonly used for:

Setting fixed widths and heights for elements.

Defining border thicknesses.

Specifying font sizes.

Positioning elements with absolute coordinates.

Example: `width: 300px;` (sets the width of an element to 300 pixels)

Advantages: Simple to understand and use. Provide precise control over element sizes.

Disadvantages: Can lead to inflexible layouts that don't adapt well to different screen sizes.

2. Percentages (%)

Definition: Percentages are relative units that are calculated based on the size of the parent element.

Usage: Percentages are often used for:

Creating fluid layouts that adapt to the browser window size.

Setting widths and heights of elements relative to their container.

Defining font sizes relative to the parent element's font size.

Example: `width: 50%;` (sets the width of an element to 50% of its parent's width)

Advantages: Create flexible and responsive layouts.

Disadvantages: Can be tricky to manage in complex layouts where nested elements have percentage-based sizes.

3. Ems (em)

Definition: Ems are relative units that are calculated based on the font size of the element itself.

Usage: Ems are commonly used for:

Setting font sizes that scale proportionally with the surrounding text.

Defining margins and padding that are relative to the font size.

Example: `font-size: 1.2em;` (sets the font size to 1.2 times the current element's font size)

Advantages: Create scalable and accessible layouts. Allow for consistent scaling of text and related spacing.

Disadvantages: Can be challenging to calculate sizes in complex nested structures where font sizes vary.

Choosing the Right Unit:

Fixed Sizes: Use pixels (`px`) when you need elements to have a specific size that doesn't change.

Responsive Layouts: Use percentages (`%`) for creating flexible layouts that adapt to different screen sizes.

Scalable Text and Spacing: Use ems (`em`) for font sizes, margins, and padding that should scale proportionally with the text.

By understanding the differences between these CSS units, you can choose the most appropriate unit for each situation and create well-structured, adaptable, and visually appealing web designs.

Chapter 4

Layout and Positioning: Structuring Web Pages

4.1 The Box Model: Content, padding, border, and margin

The CSS Box Model is a fundamental concept in web design. It's a way of visualizing how each HTML element is structured and how it takes up space on a web page. Think of every element as being like a box with four layers:

1. Content:

This is the innermost layer and contains the actual content of the element, such as text, images, or other media.

The content area's size is determined by the `width` and `height` properties.[1]

2. Padding:

This is the space between the content and the border. It acts like internal spacing within the element.

You can control the padding on all four sides of the element using the `padding` property or individual properties like `padding-top`, `padding-right`, `padding-bottom`, and `padding-left`.

3. Border:

This[2] is the line that surrounds the padding and content. It defines the outer edge of the element.

You can control the border's thickness, style (solid, dashed, etc.), and color using the `border` property or individual properties like `border-width`, `border-style`, and `border-color`.

4. Margin:

This is the outermost layer and represents the space outside the border. It creates separation between the element and other elements on the page.

You can control the margin on all four sides of the element using the `margin` property or individual properties like `margin-top`, `margin-right`, `margin-bottom`, and `margin-left`.

Visualizing the Box Model:

Imagine a picture frame.

The picture itself is the **content**.

The matting around the picture is the **padding**.

The frame itself is the **border**.

The space between the frame and the wall is the **margin**.

Important Considerations:

Calculating Total Element Size: By default, the total width and height of an element are calculated by adding the content width/height, padding, and border. This can sometimes lead to unexpected layout issues.

`box-sizing` **Property:** You can use the `box-sizing` property to change how the width and height are calculated.

`box-sizing: content-box;` (default): Width and height apply only to the content area.

`box-sizing: border-box;` : Width and height include padding and border. This is often preferred for easier layout management.

Example:

CSS

```css
div {
  width: 200px;
  height: 100px;
  padding: 20px;
  border: 5px solid black;
  margin: 30px;
  box-sizing: border-box;
}
```

In this example, the `div` element will have a total width of 200px and a total height of 100px (including padding and border). The margin will create 30px of space around the element.

Understanding the CSS Box Model is crucial for creating well-structured and predictable layouts in web design. It allows you to control the spacing and dimensions of elements precisely and avoid unexpected layout issues.

4.2 Display property: Inline, block, and inline-block.

The `display` property in CSS is fundamental for controlling how elements are rendered on a web page. It determines the type of box an element generates and how it interacts with surrounding elements. Here's a breakdown of the three most common values: `inline`, `block`, and `inline-block`:

1. `inline`

Behavior:

Flows with the text content, like a word or an image within a sentence.

Does not start on a new line.

Only takes up as much width as necessary to contain its content.

Ignores `width` and `height` properties.

Vertical margins and padding have no effect on surrounding content.

Example Elements: `<span>`, `<a>`, `<img>`, `<strong>`

Use Cases:

Styling small elements within a line of text (e.g., highlighting a word, adding an icon).

Creating links within paragraphs.

2. `block`

Behavior:

Starts on a new line.

Takes up the full width available by default (stretches to the edges of its container).

Respects `width` and `height` properties.

Vertical margins and padding push other elements away.

Example Elements: `<div>`, `<p>`, `<h1>-<h6>`, `<ul>`, `<ol>`, `<form>`

Use Cases:

Creating larger structural blocks of content (e.g., paragraphs, headings, lists).

Defining layout sections within a page.

3. `inline-block`

Behavior:

Flows with the text content like `inline` elements.

Can have `width` and `height` properties applied (unlike `inline`).

Respects margins and padding on all sides (unlike `inline`).

Use Cases:

Creating a series of boxes that wrap like text (e.g., navigation menus, image galleries).

Aligning elements horizontally within a line.

Example:

HTML

```
<p>This is an <span>inline</span> element.</p>
<div>This is a block element.</div>
<span style="display: inline-block; width: 100px;
height: 50px; background-color: lightblue;">This
is an inline-block element.</span>
```

In this example:

"inline" will flow within the paragraph text.

"This is a block element." will appear on a new line and take up the full width.

The blue box ("inline-block") will flow with the text but have a defined width and height.

By understanding these `display` values, you can control the layout and flow of your web page content effectively.

4.3 Positioning elements: Static, relative, absolute, and fixed.

The `position` property in CSS is a powerful tool for controlling the layout of elements on your web page. It allows you to take elements out of the normal document flow and position them in specific ways. Here's a breakdown of the four main positioning values:

1. `static`

Default behavior: Every HTML element has `position: static` by default.

Characteristics:

Elements are positioned according to the normal flow of the document (where they appear in the HTML).

Properties like `top`, `right`, `bottom`, and `left` have no effect on statically positioned elements.

2. `relative`

Characteristics:

The element is positioned relative to its *original* position in the document flow.

You can use `top`, `right`, `bottom`, and `left` to offset the element from its original position.

Other elements in the document flow are not affected by the element's new position (they still act as if the element were in its original place).

3. `absolute`

Characteristics:

The element is completely removed from the normal document flow.

It is positioned relative to its nearest *positioned ancestor* (an ancestor element that has `position: relative`, `absolute`, or `fixed`). If there is no positioned ancestor, it's positioned relative to the initial containing block (usually the `<html>` element).

You use `top`, `right`, `bottom`, and `left` to position the element relative to its containing block.

Other elements in the document flow behave as if the absolutely positioned element doesn't exist.

4. `fixed`

Characteristics:

The element is removed from the document flow.

It is positioned relative to the *viewport* (the browser window).

The element stays in the same position even when the page is scrolled.

You use `top`, `right`, `bottom`, and `left` to position the element relative to the viewport.

Example:

HTML

```
<div style="position: relative; width: 300px;
height: 200px; border: 1px solid black;">

  This is a relative div.

    <div style="position: absolute; top: 20px;
left: 50px; background-color: yellow;">

    This is an absolute div.

  </div>

</div>
```

In this example:

The outer `div` is positioned `relative` to its normal position in the document flow.

The inner `div` is positioned `absolute`ly 20px from the top and 50px from the left of its parent (`relative`) div.

Use Cases:

`relative`: Fine-tuning the position of an element within its normal flow, creating overlapping elements.

`absolute`: Positioning elements within a specific container, creating pop-ups or tooltips.

`fixed`: Creating elements that stay in a fixed position on the screen, such as navigation bars or "back-to-top" buttons.

By understanding these positioning values, you can create complex and dynamic layouts that go beyond the limitations of the normal document flow.

Chapter 5

Typography and Text Styling: Mastering the Art of Text

5.1 Font families and web safe fonts

When it comes to typography on the web, font families and web safe fonts play a crucial role in the readability and visual appeal of your content.[1]

Font Families

A font family is a set of fonts that share common design characteristics.[2] They are categorized into five main types:[3]

1 Serif: These fonts have small lines or "feet" at the ends of the strokes.[4] They are generally considered more traditional and are often used for body text in printed materials.[5] Examples: Times New Roman, Georgia, Garamond.[6]

2 Sans-serif: These fonts lack the serifs.[7] They have a cleaner, more modern look and are often used for headings and online content.[8] Examples: Arial, Helvetica, Verdana.[9]

3 Monospace: In these fonts, every character occupies the same amount of horizontal space.[10] They are often used for code and data display.[11] Examples: Courier, Courier New, Monaco.[12]

4 Cursive: These fonts mimic handwriting, with flowing strokes and connected letters.[13] They are often used for decorative purposes.[14] Examples: Brush Script MT, Lucida Handwriting.[15]

5 Fantasy: These fonts are decorative and often highly stylized.[16] They are used sparingly for specific design effects. Examples: Impact, Papyrus.

Web Safe Fonts

Web safe fonts are fonts that are pre-installed on most operating systems.[17] This means you can use them in your CSS with a high degree of confidence that they will render correctly for most users, regardless of their device or browser.

Here are some of the most common web safe fonts:

Serif:

Times New Roman[18]

Georgia[19]

Garamond[20]

Sans-serif:

Arial[21]

Helvetica[22]

Verdana[23]

Trebuchet MS[24]

Tahoma[25]

Monospace:

Courier New[26]

Courier

Lucida Console[27]

Monaco[28]

Using Fonts in CSS

To use a font in your CSS, you use the `font-family` property. You can specify a single font or a list of fonts as a fallback mechanism.[29]

CSS

```
body {
    font-family: Arial, Helvetica, sans-serif;
}
```

In this example, the browser will first try to use Arial. If Arial is not available, it will try Helvetica. If neither is available, it will use a generic sans-serif font.

Why Web Safe Fonts Matter

Consistency: Web safe fonts ensure that your website looks consistent across different devices and browsers.[30]

Performance: Using web safe fonts can improve page load times because the browser doesn't need to download external font files.[31]

Accessibility: Using common fonts can make your website more accessible to users with visual impairments or reading difficulties.

Beyond Web Safe Fonts

While web safe fonts are a reliable option, you can also use a wider range of fonts by using web fonts (fonts that are downloaded from a server) or by embedding fonts directly into your website. Services like Google Fonts provide a vast library of free web fonts that you can easily incorporate into your designs.[32]

5.2 Text properties: Size, weight, style, and color.

CSS provides a rich set of properties to control the visual appearance of text content on your web pages. Here's a breakdown of some essential text properties:

1. `font-size`

Purpose: Sets the size of the font.

Values:

Absolute units: `px` (pixels), `pt` (points), `cm` (centimeters), `mm` (millimeters), `in` (inches)

Relative units: `em` (relative to the parent element's font size), `rem` (relative to the root element's font size), `%` (percentage of the parent element's font size)

Example: `font-size: 16px;`, `font-size: 1.2em;`

2. `font-weight`

Purpose: Sets the weight (boldness) of the font.

Values:

Keywords: `normal`, `bold`, `bolder`, `lighter`

Numerical values: 100 (thin) to 900 (black)

Example: `font-weight: bold;`, `font-weight: 700;`

3. `font-style`

Purpose: Sets the style of the font.

Values: `normal`, `italic`, `oblique`

Example: `font-style: italic;`

4. color

Purpose: Sets the color of the text.

Values:

Color names: red, blue, green, etc.

Hexadecimal codes: #ff0000, #0000ff, etc.

RGB values: rgb(255, 0, 0), rgb(0, 0, 255), etc.

HSL values: hsl(0, 100%, 50%), hsl(240, 100%, 50%), etc.

Example: color: blue;, color: #ff0000;

5. text-align

Purpose: Aligns the text within its containing element.

Values: left, center, right, justify

Example: text-align: center;

6. line-height

Purpose: Sets the vertical spacing between lines of text.

Values: Numbers (unitless, px, em, etc.), percentages

Example: line-height: 1.5;

7. text-decoration

Purpose: Adds decorations to the text.

Values: none, underline, overline, line-through

Example: text-decoration: underline;

8. text-transform

Purpose: Controls the capitalization of the text.

Values: none, uppercase, lowercase, capitalize

Example: text-transform: uppercase;

Example:

CSS

```
h1 {
    font-size: 2em;
    font-weight: bold;
    color: #333;
    text-align: center;
}

p {
    font-size: 16px;
    line-height: 1.5;
    color: #666;
}
```

This CSS code styles `<h1>` elements with a large, bold font, dark gray color, and centered alignment. It also styles `<p>` elements with a 16px font size, 1.5 line height, and a lighter gray color.

By using these text properties effectively, you can create visually appealing and readable content that enhances the user experience on your website.

5.3 Line height, letter spacing, and text alignment.

These CSS properties are essential for controlling the visual spacing and arrangement of text content, making it more readable and aesthetically pleasing.[1] Here's a breakdown of each:

1. Line Height (`line-height`)

Purpose: Controls the vertical space between lines of text.[2] It affects the readability and visual appeal of paragraphs and blocks of text.[3]

Values:

`normal` (default): Lets the browser determine the line height.

Number (unitless): Multiplies the element's font size (e.g., `line-height: 1.5` is 1.5 times the font size).

Length units: `px`, `em`, `rem`, etc. (e.g., `line-height: 20px`).

Percentage: Percentage of the element's font size (e.g., `line-height: 150%`).

Example:

CSS

```
p {
  font-size: 16px;
    line-height: 1.5;  /* Results in 24px line
height */
}
```

Impact on Readability:

Too tight (small line height): Makes text cramped and difficult to read.[4]

Too loose (large line height): Makes text feel disjointed and can disrupt the flow.[5]

Ideal line height: Generally around 1.4 to 1.6 times the font size for body text.

2. Letter Spacing (`letter-spacing`)

Purpose: Controls the space between individual characters (letters) in a text.[6] It can be used to improve readability or create stylistic effects.[7]

Values:

`normal` (default): Uses the browser's default letter spacing.

Length units: `px`, `em`, `rem`, etc. (positive values increase spacing, negative values decrease spacing).[8]

Example:

CSS

```
h1 {
    letter-spacing: 2px;  /* Adds 2px of space
between letters */
```

```
}
```

Use Cases:

Improving readability of condensed or small fonts.[9]

Creating visual emphasis or a specific design aesthetic.

3. Text Alignment (`text-align`)

Purpose: Controls how text is aligned horizontally within its containing element.[10]

Values:

`left` (default for left-to-right languages): Aligns text to the left.

`right`: Aligns text to the right.

`center`: Centers the text.

`justify`: Stretches lines of text to fill the width of the container (except for the last line).

Example:

CSS

```css
p {
  text-align: justify;
}
```

Impact on Layout:

Affects the visual flow and balance of text content.

Can be used to create different visual effects and hierarchy.[11]

By carefully adjusting line height, letter spacing, and text alignment, you can optimize the readability and visual presentation of your text content, creating a more engaging and user-friendly experience.

Chapter 6

Colors and Backgrounds: Adding Visual Interest

6.1 Color theory and web color palettes.

Color is a powerful tool in web design.[1] It can evoke emotions, influence user behavior, and create a strong visual impact.[2] Understanding color theory and how to create effective web color palettes is crucial for designing engaging and visually appealing websites.[3]

Color Theory Basics

Color theory is a set of principles that guide the use of color in design.[4] Here are some key concepts:

Color Wheel: The color wheel is a visual representation of colors arranged according to their chromatic relationship.[5] It's a helpful tool for understanding color harmonies and creating palettes.[6]

Primary Colors: Red, yellow, and blue.[7] These colors cannot be created by mixing other colors.[8]

Secondary Colors: Created by mixing two primary colors (e.g., green, orange, violet).[9]

Tertiary Colors: Created by mixing a primary color with a neighboring secondary color (e.g., red-violet, blue-green).[10]

Hue: The pure spectrum colors, commonly referred to by color names (red, blue, green, etc.).[11]

Saturation: The intensity or purity of a color.[12] High saturation means a vivid color, low saturation means a muted color.

Value (Brightness): The lightness or darkness of a color.[13]

Color Harmonies

Color harmonies are combinations of colors that create a sense of visual balance and appeal.[14] Some common color harmonies include:

Complementary: Colors that are opposite each other on the color wheel (e.g., red and green).[15] They create high contrast and visual impact.[16]

Analogous: Colors that are adjacent to each other on the color wheel (e.g., blue, blue-green, green).[17] They create a sense of harmony and unity.

Triadic: Three colors that are evenly spaced around the color wheel (e.g., red, yellow, blue).[18] They offer a balanced and vibrant palette.

Monochromatic: Variations of a single hue, using different tints, tones, and shades.[19] They create a subtle and elegant look.

Creating Web Color Palettes

1 Choose a Base Color: Start with a main color that reflects the overall mood and purpose of your website.[20] Consider your brand identity and target audience.

2 Select Supporting Colors: Use color theory principles (complementary, analogous, etc.) to choose colors that harmonize with your base color.[21]

3 Consider Color Psychology: Different colors evoke different emotions and associations.[22] For example, blue is often associated with trust and calmness, while red can convey excitement or urgency.[23]

4 Use a Color Palette Generator: Tools like Adobe Color, Coolors, and Paletton can help you generate color palettes based on different color harmonies.[24]

5 Test Your Palette: Ensure your color palette works well in different contexts and on different devices. Check for accessibility (sufficient contrast for users with visual impairments).

Tips for Web Color Palettes

Limit the Number of Colors: Use a small number of colors (3-5) to avoid visual clutter and maintain a cohesive design.[25]

Use Neutral Colors: Incorporate neutral colors (white, black, gray, beige) to create balance and visual hierarchy.[26]

Consider Accessibility: Ensure sufficient color contrast between text and background for readability.

Be Consistent: Use your color palette consistently throughout your website to create a unified brand identity.

By understanding color theory and using effective color palettes, you can create visually engaging and user-friendly websites that leave a lasting impression on visitors.[27]

6.2 Background colors, images, and gradients.

Backgrounds play a crucial role in web design, providing visual interest, setting the mood, and enhancing the overall user experience. CSS offers several ways to style backgrounds, including colors, images, and gradients.

1. Background Colors

`background-color` **property:** Sets the background color of an element.

Values:

Color names (e.g., `red`, `blue`, `green`)

Hexadecimal codes (e.g., `#ff0000`, `#0000ff`)

RGB values (e.g., `rgb(255, 0, 0)`, `rgb(0, 0, 255)`)

HSL values (e.g., `hsl(0, 100%, 50%)`, `hsl(240, 100%, 50%)`)

`transparent` (no color)

Example:

CSS

```
body {
    background-color: #f0f0f0;  /* Light gray
background */
}
```

2. Background Images

`background-image` **property:** Sets an image as the background of an element.

Value: `url("path/to/image.jpg")`

Example:

CSS

```
header {
  background-image: url("images/banner.jpg");
}
```

Additional Properties:

`background-repeat`: Controls how the image repeats (e.g., `repeat`, `repeat-x`, `repeat-y`, `no-repeat`).

background-position: Specifies the position of the image within the element (e.g., center, top left, bottom right, percentages, pixels).

background-size: Controls the size of the background image (e.g., cover, contain, 100px, 50%).

background-attachment: Determines whether the background image scrolls with the page or stays fixed (e.g., scroll, fixed).

3. Background Gradients

background-image **property:** Used to create gradients as backgrounds.

Values:

linear-gradient(): Creates a linear gradient that transitions between two or more colors along a straight line.

radial-gradient(): Creates a radial gradient that transitions between colors radiating from a central point.

Example:

CSS

```
div {
    background-image: linear-gradient(to right,
red, yellow); /* Gradient from red to yellow */
}
```

Gradient Syntax:

Direction: to top, to bottom, to left, to right, or an angle (e.g., 45deg).

Color stops: Define the colors and their positions within the gradient (e.g., `red`, `yellow 50%`, `blue 100%`).

Combining Background Properties

You can combine multiple background properties to create layered effects. For example:

CSS

```
div {
    background-color:    #f0f0f0;   /*   Light   gray
background color */
  background-image:
          url("images/pattern.png"),   /*    Tiled
background image */
    linear-gradient(to bottom, #e0e0e0, #ffffff);
/* Gradient overlay */
  background-repeat: repeat, no-repeat; /* Repeat
pattern, no repeat for gradient */
}
```

By using background colors, images, and gradients effectively, you can create visually rich and engaging web pages that capture the attention of your visitors.

6.3 Opacity and transparency effects.

Opacity and transparency effects are powerful tools in CSS that allow you to control the visibility of elements and create interesting visual effects.[1] They are often used to create overlays, fade-in/fade-out animations, and subtle design elements.[2]

Opacity

`opacity` **property:** Controls the overall opacity of an element.[3]

Values:

`1` (or `100%`): Fully opaque (default).

`0` (or `0%`): Fully transparent (invisible).

Values between `0` and `1`: Partially transparent (e.g., `0.5` for 50% opacity).

Effect: Opacity affects the element and all its children.[4] If you set the opacity of a parent element, all its child elements will also become partially transparent.[5]

Example:

CSS

```
div {
  opacity: 0.7; /* 70% opacity */
}
```

Transparency

While the term "transparency" is often used interchangeably with "opacity," in CSS, it specifically refers to the `background-color` property with an `rgba()` or `hsla()` value.

`rgba()` **and** `hsla()`: These color functions allow you to specify a color with an alpha channel, which controls the transparency of the color.[6]

Syntax:

```
rgba(red, green, blue, alpha)

hsla(hue, saturation, lightness, alpha)
```

Alpha value:

1: Fully opaque.

0: Fully transparent.

Values between 0 and 1: Partially transparent.

Example:

CSS

```
div {
    background-color: rgba(255, 0, 0, 0.5); /* Red
with 50% transparency */
}
```

Key Differences and Use Cases

Opacity: Affects the entire element, including its content and background. Useful for creating fading effects or overlays where you want the entire element to be semi-transparent.

Transparency (with rgba()/hsla()**):** Affects only the background color of the element. Useful for creating backgrounds that blend with their surroundings or allowing content to be visible through a semi-transparent background.

Example: Image Overlay

CSS

```css
.image-container {
  position: relative;
}

.image-overlay {
  position: absolute;
  top: 0;
  left: 0;
  width: 100%;
  height: 100%;
  background-color: rgba(0, 0,[7] 0, 0.5); /* Black
overlay with 50%[8] opacity */
  color: white;
  text-align: center;
}
```

This CSS creates a semi-transparent black overlay on top of an image, allowing text to be displayed on top of the image with good readability.

By understanding opacity and transparency, you can add depth and visual interest to your web designs, creating more engaging and user-friendly experiences.[9]

Chapter 7

Working with Images: Optimizing for the Web

7.1 Image formats: JPEG, PNG, and GIF.

When adding images to your web pages, choosing the right image format is crucial for balancing image quality, file size, and performance. Here's a breakdown of the three most common web image formats: JPEG, PNG, and GIF.

1. JPEG (Joint Photographic Experts Group)

Compression: Lossy compression (some image data is discarded to reduce file size).

Best for:

Photographs and images with complex colors and details.

Images where a slight loss of quality is acceptable.

Pros:

Smaller file sizes, which lead to faster loading times.

Wide browser support.

Cons:

Loss of image quality with repeated editing and saving.

Doesn't support transparency.

2. PNG (Portable Network Graphics)

Compression: Lossless compression (no image data is lost).

Best for:

Images with sharp lines, text, and graphics (e.g., logos, illustrations).

Images that require transparency.

Pros:

High image quality.

Supports transparency (with alpha channel for varying levels of transparency).

Cons:

Larger file sizes compared to JPEG, which can affect loading times.

3. GIF (Graphics Interchange Format)

Compression: Lossless compression.

Best for:

Simple animations.

Images with limited colors (up to 256 colors).

Pros:

Supports simple animations.

Small file sizes for images with limited colors.

Cons:

Limited color palette (not suitable for photographs).

Not ideal for images with complex details.

Choosing the Right Format

Here's a quick guide to help you choose the best format:

Photographs: JPEG

Logos and graphics: PNG

Animations: GIF

Images with transparency: PNG

Small file size is a priority: JPEG

High image quality is a priority: PNG

Optimizing Images

Regardless of the format you choose, it's important to optimize your images for the web:

Resize images: Use the appropriate dimensions for your web page to avoid unnecessarily large images.

Compress images: Use image optimization tools to reduce file size without significant loss of quality.

Use the `alt` **attribute:** Provide descriptive alternative text for all images to improve accessibility and SEO.

By understanding the strengths and weaknesses of each image format and optimizing your images, you can ensure that your web pages load quickly and provide a great visual experience for your visitors.

7.2 Image attributes: Alt text, width, and height.

You're right to focus on image attributes! They provide important information about images and how they should be displayed on your web pages. Here's a breakdown of three essential image attributes:

1. `alt` (Alternative Text)

Purpose:

Accessibility: Provides a text description of the image for users who are visually impaired and use screen readers.

SEO: Helps search engines understand the content of the image, which can improve your website's ranking.

Fallback: Displayed if the image cannot be loaded due to a broken link, slow connection, or other errors.

How to use:

HTML

```
<img src="image.jpg" alt="A descriptive text of
the image">
```

Best practices:

Be concise and descriptive.

Accurately reflect the content and purpose of the image.

Avoid keyword stuffing (for SEO purposes).

If the image is purely decorative, use an empty `alt` attribute: `alt=""`.

2. `width`

Purpose: Specifies the width of the image in pixels.

How to use:

HTML

```
<img    src="image.jpg"    alt="Image    description"
width="300">
```

This will display the image with a width of 300 pixels.

Responsive images: It's generally recommended to use CSS to control image dimensions for responsiveness. However, the `width` attribute can still be useful in some cases, especially when combined with the `height` attribute to maintain aspect ratio.

3. `height`

Purpose: Specifies the height of the image in pixels.

How to use:

HTML

```
<img    src="image.jpg"    alt="Image    description"
height="200">
```

This will display the image with a height of 200 pixels.

Responsive images: Similar to the `width` attribute, it's generally best to use CSS for responsive height control.

Important notes:

Aspect ratio: When specifying both `width` and `height`, the browser will try to maintain the image's aspect ratio. If you only specify one dimension, the browser will automatically adjust the other dimension to maintain the aspect ratio.

CSS for responsiveness: For responsive images that adapt to different screen sizes, it's recommended to use CSS and techniques like `max-width: 100%;` and `height: auto;` to ensure images scale proportionally.

By using these image attributes effectively, you can improve the accessibility, SEO, and visual presentation of your web pages.

7.3 Responsive images: Adapting to different screen sizes.

Responsive images are a crucial aspect of modern web design. They ensure that your images look great and function properly on any device, regardless of screen size or resolution. Here's a breakdown of why they matter and how to implement them:

Why Responsive Images are Important

User Experience: Images that are too large or too small can create a frustrating user experience. Responsive images adapt to the user's device, providing optimal viewing and interaction.

Performance: Serving large images to small screens wastes bandwidth and slows down page load times. Responsive images deliver appropriately sized images, improving website performance.

SEO: Search engines favor websites that provide a good user experience across all devices. Responsive images contribute to better SEO rankings.

Techniques for Responsive Images

`max-width: 100%;` **and** `height: auto;`

This simple CSS technique allows images to scale down proportionally to fit their container while maintaining their aspect ratio.

Example:

CSS

```css
img {
  max-width: 100%;
  height: auto;
}
```

The `<picture>` **element**

This HTML5 element provides a more flexible way to specify different image sources based on media queries (conditions based on screen size, resolution, etc.).

Example:

HTML

```
<picture>
        <source    media="(min-width:    768px)"
srcset="image-large.jpg">
        <source    media="(min-width:    480px)"
srcset="image-medium.jpg">
        <img   src="image-small.jpg"   alt="Image
description">
</picture>
```

This code will display `image-large.jpg` on screens wider than 768px, `image-medium.jpg` on screens wider than 480px, and `image-small.jpg` as the default.

srcset and sizes attributes

These attributes on the `<img>` tag allow you to provide multiple image sources with different resolutions and let the browser choose the most appropriate one based on screen size and resolution.

Example:

HTML

```
<img src="image-small.jpg"
     alt="Image description"
     srcset="image-small.jpg 480w,
             image-medium.jpg 768w,
             image-large.jpg 1200w"
     sizes="(max-width: 480px) 100vw,
            (max-width: 768px) 50vw,
            33vw">
```

This code provides three image sources with different widths and uses the `sizes` attribute to tell the browser how much space the image should occupy on different screen sizes.

Client-side image optimization tools

Services like Cloudinary and Imgix can automatically optimize and deliver responsive images based on user context (device, screen size, network conditions).

Key Considerations

Art direction: Sometimes you need more than just resizing; you might need to crop or use different images entirely for different screen sizes to ensure the most important content is visible.

Performance: Always optimize your images for the web to minimize file sizes and improve loading times.

Accessibility: Don't forget to use descriptive `alt` text for all images to ensure accessibility for users with visual impairments.

By implementing responsive images, you can create a more user-friendly, performant, and accessible web experience for your visitors, no matter what device they are using.

Chapter 8

Responsive Web Design: Creating Mobile-Friendly Websites

8.1 Media queries: Targeting different devices.

Media queries are a powerful CSS feature that allows you to apply different styles based on the characteristics of the device[1] being used to view your website. This enables you to create responsive designs that adapt seamlessly to various screen sizes, orientations, and resolutions.

How Media Queries Work

Media queries use the `@media` rule followed by a condition and a set of CSS rules. The styles within a media query are applied only when the condition is met.

Syntax:

CSS

```
@media (condition) {
    /* CSS rules to apply when the condition is
true */
}
```

Common Media Features

`width`: Targets the width of the viewport (browser window).

`min-width`: Applies styles when the viewport width is at least the specified value.

`max-width`: Applies styles when the viewport width is at most the specified value.

`height`: Targets the height of the viewport.

`min-height`: Applies styles when the viewport height is at least the specified value.

`max-height`: Applies styles when the viewport height is at most the specified value.

`orientation`: Targets the orientation of the device (portrait or landscape).

`resolution`: Targets the resolution of the screen (dots per inch or dpi).

`aspect-ratio`: Targets the aspect ratio of the viewport.

Example

CSS

```css
/* Styles for smaller screens (e.g., mobile
phones) */
@media (max-width: 768px) {
  body {
    font-size: 14px;
  }
  nav ul {
    display: none; /* Hide the navigation menu */
  }
}
```

```
/* Styles for larger screens (e.g., tablets and
desktops) */
@media (min-width: 769px) {
  body {
    font-size: 16px;
  }
  nav ul {
      display: block; /* Show the navigation menu
*/
  }
}
```

In this example:

On screens with a maximum width of 768px, the font size is set to 14px, and the navigation menu is hidden.

On screens with a minimum width of 769px, the font size is set to 16px, and the navigation menu is displayed.

Benefits of Media Queries

Responsive Design: Create websites that adapt to different screen sizes and devices.

Improved User Experience: Ensure optimal viewing and interaction on any device.

Increased Accessibility: Cater to users with different needs and preferences.

SEO Benefits: Search engines favor websites that are mobile-friendly and responsive.

Using Media Queries Effectively

Mobile-First Approach: Start by designing for the smallest screen size and then progressively add styles for larger screens using media queries with `min-width`.

Breakpoints: Identify key screen sizes (breakpoints) where your layout needs to change significantly.

Testing: Test your website on different devices and screen sizes to ensure it looks and functions as expected.

By mastering media queries, you can create dynamic and adaptable websites that provide a great user experience across all devices.

8.2 Fluid layouts and flexible images.

Fluid layouts and flexible images are essential components of responsive web design, ensuring that your website adapts seamlessly to different screen sizes and devices.

Fluid Layouts

Fluid layouts use relative units like percentages instead of fixed units like pixels to define the width of elements. This allows the layout to adjust smoothly to the available screen space.

Key characteristics:

Proportional scaling: Elements resize proportionally to their parent container.

Flexibility: The layout adapts to various screen sizes without breaking or requiring horizontal scrolling.

Improved user experience: Content is easily readable and accessible on any device.

Implementation:

Use percentages for widths: Instead of `width: 500px;`, use `width: 50%;`.

Avoid fixed-width elements: Minimize the use of elements with fixed widths that can restrict the flexibility of the layout.

Use CSS layout tools: Modern CSS layout tools like Flexbox and Grid make it easier to create fluid and responsive layouts.

Flexible Images

Flexible images are designed to scale proportionally with their container, preventing them from overflowing or breaking the layout.

Key characteristics:

Maintain aspect ratio: Images scale proportionally without distortion.

Prevent overflow: Images never exceed the width of their container.

Improve performance: Smaller images are loaded on smaller screens, improving page load times.

Implementation:

`max-width: 100%;` **and** `height: auto;`**:** This CSS rule allows images to scale down as needed while maintaining their aspect ratio.

The `<picture>` **element:** This HTML5 element allows you to specify different image sources for different screen sizes.

`srcset` **and** `sizes` **attributes:** These attributes on the `<img>` tag enable you to provide multiple image sources with different resolutions, letting the browser choose the best one.

Benefits of Fluid Layouts and Flexible Images

Enhanced user experience: Content is accessible and visually appealing on all devices.

Improved performance: Faster loading times, especially on mobile devices.

SEO benefits: Search engines favor websites that are mobile-friendly and responsive.

Future-proof design: As new devices with different screen sizes emerge, your website will be able to adapt.

Example

HTML

```html
<!DOCTYPE html>
<html>
<head>
  <style>
    .container {
      max-width: 960px;
      margin: 0 auto;
    }
    img {
      max-width: 100%;
      height: auto;
    }
  </style>
</head>
<body>
  <div class="container">
        <img src="image.jpg" alt="A responsive image">
  </div>
</body>
</html>
```

In this example:

The `.container` has a `max-width` to prevent it from becoming too wide on large screens.

The `img` has `max-width: 100%;` and `height: auto;` to ensure it scales proportionally within its container.

By combining fluid layouts and flexible images, you can create a truly responsive website that provides a consistent and enjoyable experience for all users, regardless of their device.

8.3 Mobile-first design principles.

Mobile-first design is a philosophy that prioritizes the user experience on mobile devices above all else. It's about starting your design process with the smallest screen and the most limited resources in mind, then progressively enhancing the experience for larger screens. This approach has become increasingly important as mobile devices have overtaken desktops as the primary way people access the internet.

Here are the key principles of mobile-first design:

1. Content Prioritization

Focus on essential content: Identify the core information and functionalities that users need on mobile and prioritize them.

Streamline content: Remove any unnecessary elements or distractions that don't contribute to the core purpose of the page.

Progressive disclosure: Reveal additional content or features as needed based on user interactions or screen size.

2. Simplified Navigation

Concise menus: Use clear and concise labels for navigation items.

Prioritize key actions: Make the most important actions easily accessible.

Consider touch targets: Ensure buttons and links are large enough and spaced appropriately for touch interactions.

3. Optimized Performance

Minimize file sizes: Optimize images, scripts, and other assets to reduce loading times.

Efficient code: Use clean and efficient HTML, CSS, and JavaScript to improve performance.

Caching: Leverage browser caching to store frequently accessed resources.

4. Readability and Typography

Legible fonts: Choose fonts that are easy to read on small screens.

Appropriate font sizes: Ensure text is large enough to be comfortable to read without zooming.

Sufficient contrast: Use good color contrast between text and background for readability.

5. Touch-Friendly Design

Touch targets: Make interactive elements large enough and spaced appropriately for touch input.

Gestures: Consider using touch gestures (tap, swipe, pinch) for common actions.

Avoid hover states: Hover effects are not relevant on touch devices.

Benefits of Mobile-First Design

Improved user experience: Creates a better experience for the growing number of mobile users.

Enhanced performance: Leads to faster loading times and better overall performance.

Cost-effectiveness: It's often more efficient to design for mobile first and then scale up, rather than the other way around.

Better SEO: Search engines prioritize mobile-friendly websites.

Future-proof design: As mobile usage continues to grow, a mobile-first approach ensures your website is ready for the future.

Implementing Mobile-First

Start with the smallest screen: Begin your design process by considering the mobile experience first.

Use a mobile-first CSS framework: Frameworks like Bootstrap and Foundation are designed with mobile-first principles in mind.

Test thoroughly: Test your website on a variety of real mobile devices to ensure it works as expected.

By embracing mobile-first design principles, you can create websites that are user-friendly, performant, and accessible to everyone, regardless of the device they are using.

Chapter 9

Forms and User Input: Interactive Web Pages

9.1 Creating forms with various input types.

HTML forms are essential for collecting user input on websites. They allow users to submit data like text, passwords, selections, and files. The `<input>` element is the backbone of forms, and it offers a variety of `type` attributes to create different input fields. Here's a breakdown of some common input types:

1. Text Input

`type="text"`: Creates a single-line text box for short text input (e.g., names, addresses).

Example:

HTML

```
<label for="name">Name:</label>
<input type="text" id="name" name="name">
```

2. Password Input

`type="password"`: Creates a text box where the characters are masked (e.g., for passwords).

Example:

HTML

```
<label for="password">Password:</label>
<input        type="password"        id="password"
name="password">
```

3. Email Input

`type="email"`: Creates a text box specifically for email addresses. Some browsers may perform basic validation.

Example:

HTML

```
<label for="email">Email:</label>
<input type="email" id="email" name="email">
```

4. Number Input

`type="number"`: Creates a field for entering numbers. Often includes up/down arrows for incrementing/decrementing.

Example:

HTML

```
<label for="quantity">Quantity:</label>
<input        type="number"        id="quantity"
name="quantity" min="1" max="10">
```

5. Radio Buttons

`type="radio"`: Creates a set of radio buttons where only one option can be selected.

Example:

HTML

```
<label for="male">Male</label>
<input   type="radio"   id="male"   name="gender"
value="male">
<label for="female">Female</label>
<input   type="radio"   id="female"   name="gender"
value="female">[1]
```

6. Checkboxes

type="checkbox": Creates a checkbox that allows users to select multiple options.

Example:

HTML

```
<label for="html">HTML</label>
<input   type="checkbox"   id="html"   name="skills"
value="html">
<label for="css">CSS</label>
<input   type="checkbox"   id="css"   name="skills"
value="css">[2]
```

7. Submit Button

type="submit": Creates a button that submits the form data to the server.

Example:

HTML

```
<input type="submit" value="Submit">
```

8. File Input

`type="file"`: Creates a field for uploading files.

Example:

HTML

```
<label for="file">Upload file:</label>
<input type="file" id="file" name="file">
```

9. Date Input

`type="date"`: Creates a calendar picker for selecting dates.

Example:

HTML

```
<label for="date">Date:</label>
<input type="date" id="date" name="date">
```

10. Hidden Input

`type="hidden"`: Creates a hidden field that is not visible to the user but can be used to send data to the server.

Example:

HTML

```
<input type="hidden" name="user_id" value="123">
```

Important Considerations:

Labels (`<label>`): Use labels to associate text with input fields, improving usability and accessibility.

Name attribute: The `name` attribute is essential for identifying the input data when the form is submitted.

Validation: Use HTML5 validation attributes (e.g., `required`, `pattern`, `min`, `max`) and/or JavaScript to ensure data is valid before submission.

By using various input types and following best practices, you can create user-friendly and effective forms that collect the information you need.

9.2 Form styling and validation.

Form Styling

CSS provides extensive control over the appearance of form elements, allowing you to create visually appealing and user-friendly forms that integrate seamlessly with your website's design.

Key areas for styling:

Overall form container: Style the `<form>` element itself to control its width, padding, borders, and background.

Input fields: Style the `<input>`, `<textarea>`, and `<select>` elements to control their size, borders, colors, fonts, and spacing.

Labels: Style the `<label>` elements to ensure clear association with input fields and improve readability.

Buttons: Style the `<button>` or `<input type="submit">` elements to create visually appealing and interactive buttons.

Error messages: Style error messages to provide clear visual feedback to users.

CSS properties for form styling:

Basic properties: width, height, padding, margin, border, background-color, color, font-family, font-size

Focus state: :focus pseudo-class to style elements when they are selected.

Hover state: :hover pseudo-class to style elements when the mouse hovers over them.

Disabled state: :disabled pseudo-class to style disabled elements.

Form validation pseudo-classes: :valid and :invalid to style elements based on their validation status.

Example:

CSS

```css
form {
  width: 300px;
  padding: 20px;
  border: 1px solid #ccc;
}

input[type="text"],
input[type="email"],
textarea {
  width: 100%;
  padding: 10px;
  margin-bottom: 10px;
  border: 1px solid #ccc;
}
```

```
input[type="submit"] {
  background-color: #007bff;¹
  color: white;
  padding: 10px 20px;
  border: none;
  cursor: pointer;²
}
```

Form Validation

Form validation is the process of checking user input to ensure it meets certain criteria before it is submitted to the server. This helps prevent errors, protects against security vulnerabilities, and improves the user experience.

Types of form validation:

Client-side validation: Performed in the user's browser using JavaScript. It provides immediate feedback to the user.

Server-side validation: Performed on the server after the form is submitted. It is essential for security and data integrity.

HTML5 validation attributes:

`required`: Specifies that a field must be filled out.

`pattern`: Specifies a regular expression that the input value must match.

`min` **and** `max`: Specify the minimum and maximum values for number and date inputs.

`minlength` **and** `maxlength`: Specify the minimum and maximum length for text inputs.

`type="email"`: Performs basic email format validation.

JavaScript validation:

JavaScript can be used to perform more complex validation and provide custom error messages.

Libraries like jQuery Validate can simplify the process of implementing JavaScript validation.

Styling validation feedback:

Use CSS pseudo-classes like `:valid` and `:invalid` to provide visual cues to the user about the validation status of input fields.

Use clear and concise error messages to guide the user towards correcting invalid input.

Example (using HTML5 and CSS):

HTML

```html
<form>
  <label for="email">Email:</label>
    <input type="email" id="email" name="email" required>
  <input type="submit" value="Submit">
</form>
```
[3]

CSS

```css
input:valid {
  border-color: green;
}
```

```
input:invalid {
  border-color: red;
}
```

By combining form styling and validation techniques, you can create user-friendly, visually appealing, and secure forms that enhance the overall user experience on your website.

9.3 Handling user data with server-side scripting (brief overview).

While HTML and CSS handle the front-end presentation of a form, server-side scripting takes over when it comes to processing and storing the data users submit. Here's a simplified overview of how that works:

1. The Form's Journey

User Input: The user fills out the form fields and clicks the submit button.

Data Sent to Server: The form data is sent to the web server where your website is hosted.

Server-Side Script Takes Over: A server-side script (written in languages like PHP, Python, Node.js, Ruby, etc.) receives the form data.

2. Processing the Data

Data Retrieval: The script accesses the submitted data, often using the `name` attributes of the form fields.

Validation (Again!): The script performs server-side validation to ensure data integrity and security, even if client-side validation was bypassed.

Data Sanitization: The script cleans the data to prevent security risks like SQL injection attacks. This might involve removing potentially harmful characters or escaping special characters.

Database Interaction: The script often interacts with a database to store the data or retrieve related information. This might involve inserting new records, updating existing ones, or performing queries.

3. Response to the User

Confirmation or Feedback: The script typically sends a response back to the user's browser, which could be:

A confirmation message ("Thank you for your submission!")

A redirection to another page (e.g., a success page or a thank you page)

An error message if there were issues with the submission

Example (Conceptual PHP)

PHP

```php
<?php
if ($_SERVER["REQUEST_METHOD"] == "POST") {
  $name = $_POST["name"];
  $email = $_POST["email"];

  // Perform validation and sanitization...

  // Connect to database...

  // Store data in the database...

  echo "Thank you for your submission!";
}
?>
```

Key Considerations

Security: Server-side scripting is crucial for secure handling of user data. Always validate and sanitize input to prevent vulnerabilities.

Database Interactions: Understanding database concepts and how to interact with them using server-side scripts is essential for many web applications.

Error Handling: Implement robust error handling to gracefully manage unexpected situations and provide informative feedback to users.

User Privacy: Handle user data responsibly and ethically, following privacy regulations and best practices.

This overview provides a basic understanding of how server-side scripting plays a vital role in handling user data submitted through forms. It's a vast topic with many nuances depending on the specific technologies and application requirements.

Chapter 10

Beyond the Basics: Advanced CSS Techniques

10.1 CSS frameworks: Bootstrap and Foundation.

CSS frameworks like Bootstrap and Foundation provide pre-written CSS and JavaScript code that simplifies and speeds up web development.[1] They offer a collection of reusable UI components, a responsive grid system, and helpful utility classes, making it easier to create consistent and visually appealing websites.[2]

Bootstrap

Developed by: Originally created by Twitter, now maintained by the open-source community.[3]

Key features:

Responsive grid system: A 12-column grid system that adapts to different screen sizes.[4]

Extensive component library: Includes pre-styled components like buttons, forms, navigation bars, modals, and more.[5]

JavaScript plugins: Provides interactive components like carousels, tooltips, and modal windows.[6]

Customization: Offers theming options and variables to customize the look and feel.[7]

Pros:

Large community and resources: Extensive documentation, tutorials, and community support.[8]

Easy to learn and use: Relatively low learning curve, especially for beginners.[9]

Wide browser compatibility: Works consistently across different browsers.[10]

Cons:

Can be bulky: The full Bootstrap framework can add significant weight to your website.[11]

Default styling: May require overriding default styles to achieve a unique look.

Foundation

Developed by: ZURB

Key features:

Flexible grid system: A customizable grid system based on Flexbox.[12]

Mobile-first approach: Prioritizes mobile design and scales up for larger screens.[13]

Semantic HTML: Emphasizes the use of semantic HTML for better structure and accessibility.[14]

Advanced features: Includes features like motion UI and rapid prototyping tools.[15]

Pros:

Customization: Offers greater flexibility and control over styling.

Accessibility: Strong focus on accessibility features.

Performance: Can be more lightweight than Bootstrap if used selectively.

Cons:

Steeper learning curve: May require more effort to learn and master.

Smaller community: Less community support and resources compared to Bootstrap.

Choosing a Framework

The choice between Bootstrap and Foundation depends on your project needs and preferences:

Bootstrap: A good choice for rapid development and projects that require a wide range of pre-built components.[16]

Foundation: A good choice for projects that prioritize customization, accessibility, and a mobile-first approach.

Alternatives

Other popular CSS frameworks include:

Bulma: A modern, Flexbox-based framework with a focus on modularity and customization.[17]

Tailwind CSS: A utility-first framework that provides a vast collection of low-level CSS classes.[18]

UIkit: A lightweight and modular framework with a clean and modern design.[19]

Key Considerations When Using Frameworks

Bloat: Be mindful of potential bloat by only including the components and features you need.

Overriding styles: Be prepared to override default styles to match your design requirements.

Learning curve: Invest time in learning the framework's grid system and components.

By leveraging the power of CSS frameworks, you can streamline your web development process, create responsive and visually appealing websites, and focus on building unique features and functionality.[20]

10.2 CSS preprocessors: Sass and Less

CSS preprocessors like Sass and Less are scripting languages that extend the functionality of regular CSS, making it easier to write maintainable, organized, and reusable stylesheets. They offer features that standard CSS lacks, such as variables, mixins, nesting, and more.

Sass (Syntactically Awesome Style Sheets)

Syntax: Uses two syntaxes:

SCSS (Sassy CSS): Uses the `.scss` file extension and has a syntax similar to CSS (with curly braces and semicolons), making it easier to learn for those familiar with CSS.

Sass (Indented Syntax): Uses the `.sass` file extension and relies on indentation to define code blocks, resulting in a more concise syntax.

Features:

Variables: Store values (colors, font sizes, etc.) in variables to reuse throughout your stylesheets.

Nesting: Nest CSS rules to reflect the structure of your HTML and improve code organization.

Mixins: Create reusable blocks of CSS code that can be included in multiple places.

Functions: Perform calculations and manipulate values within your stylesheets.

Inheritance: Extend CSS rules to create variations without repeating code.

Operators: Perform mathematical operations on values.

Example (SCSS):

SCSS

```scss
$primary-color: #007bff;

.button {
  background-color: $primary-color;
  color: white;
  padding: 10px 20px;
  border: none;

  &:hover {
        background-color:  darken($primary-color,
10%);[1]
  }
}
```

Less (Leaner Style Sheets)

Syntax: Uses a syntax similar to CSS, with curly braces and semicolons. Uses the `.less` file extension.

Features:

Variables: Similar to Sass, allows you to store and reuse values.

Mixins: Create reusable blocks of CSS code.

Nesting: Nest CSS rules for better organization.

Functions: Perform calculations and manipulate values.

Operations: Perform mathematical operations on values.

Namespaces: Group related styles into namespaces.

Example:

Less

```less
@primary-color: #007bff;

.button {
  background-color: @primary-color;
  color: white;
  padding: 10px 20px;
  border: none;

  &:hover {
        background-color:  darken(@primary-color,
10%);[2]
  }
}
```

Benefits of CSS Preprocessors

Maintainability: Improved code organization and reusability make it easier to maintain large stylesheets.

Efficiency: Reduces code repetition and makes writing CSS faster.

Readability: Nesting and variables improve the readability of CSS code.

Extensibility: Adds features that standard CSS lacks, making it more powerful.

How to Use CSS Preprocessors

CSS preprocessors require a compilation step to convert the preprocessor code into regular CSS that browsers can understand. This is usually done using a command-line tool or a task runner like Gulp or Grunt.

Choosing a Preprocessor

Both Sass and Less are powerful and popular choices. Sass is generally considered more feature-rich and has a larger community, while Less is often praised for its simplicity and ease of learning. The choice depends on your preferences and project needs.

10.3 Animations and transitions

Animations and transitions are powerful CSS techniques that bring your web pages to life by adding motion and interactivity. They can enhance user engagement, provide visual feedback, and make your website more dynamic and interesting.

Transitions

Transitions create smooth changes between two states of an element's properties over a specified duration. They are typically triggered by user interactions like hovering, clicking, or focusing on an element.

`transition` **property:** This is the shorthand property for defining transitions. It allows you to specify the properties to be animated, the duration, the timing function, and any delay.

Example:

CSS

```
.button {
```

```
  background-color: blue;
  transition: background-color 0.5s ease;
}

.button:hover {
  background-color: red;
}
```

In this example, when[1] the user hovers over the button, the background color will smoothly transition from blue to red over 0.5 seconds using an "ease" timing function.

Individual transition properties:

transition-property: Specifies the CSS property to be animated (e.g., background-color, width, opacity).

transition-duration: Specifies the duration of the transition (e.g., 0.5s, 1000ms).

transition-timing-function: Specifies the speed curve of the transition (e.g., ease, linear, ease-in-out).

transition-delay: Specifies a delay before the transition starts (e.g., 0.2s).

Animations

Animations allow you to create more complex sequences of animated changes using keyframes. They can involve multiple properties and stages, giving you greater control over the animation.

animation **property:** This is the shorthand property for defining animations. It allows you to specify the animation name, duration, timing function, delay, iteration count, direction, and fill mode.

@keyframes **rule:** This rule defines the animation sequence with keyframes that specify the styles at different points in the animation.

Example:

CSS

```css
@keyframes slideIn {
  from {
    transform: translateX(-100%);
    opacity: 0;
  }
  to {
    transform: translateX(0);
    opacity: 1;
  }
}

.box {
  animation: slideIn 1s ease-in-out;
}
```

In this example, the .box element will slide in from the left over 1 second using the slideIn animation defined with keyframes.

Individual animation properties:

`animation-name`: Specifies the name of the `@keyframes` rule.

`animation-duration`: Specifies the duration of the animation.

`animation-timing-function`: Specifies the speed curve of the animation.

`animation-delay`: Specifies a delay before the animation starts.

`animation-iteration-count`: Specifies the number of times the animation should[2] play (e.g., `infinite`). * `animation-direction`: Specifies the direction of the animation (e.g., `normal`, `reverse`, `alternate`). * `animation-fill-mode`: Specifies how the element should be styled before and after the animation (e.g., `none`, `forwards`, `backwards`, `both`).

Benefits of Animations and Transitions

Enhanced user experience: Provides visual feedback, guides user attention, and makes interactions more engaging.

Improved storytelling: Can be used to create visual narratives and guide users through content.

Visual appeal: Adds a layer of polish and sophistication to your website.

Use Cases

Hover effects on buttons and navigation items

Loading animations

Animated progress bars

Attention-grabbing banners

Interactive data visualizations

Subtle micro-interactions

By understanding and applying CSS animations and transitions, you can add a dynamic dimension to your web designs and create a more captivating experience for your users.